WALKS
BODMIN

Introduced by

E.V. THOMPSON

BOSSINEY BOOKS

We hope these pages will encourage you to explore and enjoy Bodmin Moor, but please observe the laws of courtesy and common sense and stick to routes which have rights of way, always remembering that certain parts of the moor are homes or work places.

Published by Bossiney Books
Langore, Launceston, Cornwall PL15 8LD

First published 1996
This reprint 2000

ISBN 1-899383-06-9

Acknowledgements
A number of moorland people have helped us in compiling these walks. We are also deeply indebted to Malcolm Drover of the Countryside Access Department of Cornwall County Council.

Front cover design: Maggie Ginger
Cover and modern inside photographs: Ray Bishop
Maps: Felicity Young
Drawings: Felicity Young and Donald Jackson

Printed in Great Britain by Cornwall Litho, Redruth

WALKS on BODMIN MOOR

by E V Thompson

When Michael Williams invited me to write an introduction to *Walks on Bodmin Moor*, it took me back many years. To a time when I lived on the moor and walking its wide, open spaces was an integral, and important part of my life.

It was whilst walking the moor that I gained the inspiration for my very first novel, *Chase The Wind*. This was the beginning of a love affair with Bodmin Moor that has never ended.

Chase The Wind won an international competition as the best historical novel of the year and took Bodmin Moor into the homes of very many people around the world. For them it was a glimpse into a little known and secret place. For me, it was the realisation of a lifetime's dream.

But Bodmin Moor is a place where dreams are created and fulfilled. A

ARTHUR'S Quoit near Minions is another reminder of how Arthur seems to haunt the landscape. Can there be smoke without fire?

magic place. It is also an area where the observant and receptive visitor can discover the history of mankind in Cornwall.

Visit Dozmary Pool and it is not hard to imagine primitive man squatting around its bleak shores, fashioning crude arrowheads and primitive stone tools. This is also a place of legends. These waters are reputed to be the resting place of mighty Excalibur, the sword once wielded to great effect by King Arthur of Camelot.

Similar claims are made for other places. But stand here when the wind is howling in fury as it pursues dark clouds across the moorland sky and I defy you to deny Dozmary's rightful claim to hold such a secret.

Pause on any one of a dozen Bodmin tors and you might find yourself surrounded by the faintly defined circles that once contained the homes of the early hut-dwellers. With the discovery comes realisation that the moor has not always been as empty as it is today. In fact, during the years before Christ walked the earth this would have been one of the most heavily populated areas of Cornwall. Much of it is little changed since those far-off days.

A walk on any part of Bodmin will take the visitor back in time. Visit the tiny community of Temple, little more than a hop-skip-and-a-jump from the busy A30 trunk road and you are at the very heart of the moor and of Cornish history. Once, the tiny church here was under the jurisdiction of the Knights Templars and it became Cornwall's own "Gretna Green". In the colourful early 18th-century language of the historian, Tonkin: 'Many a bad marriage-bargain is here yearly slubbered up. 'The little church has been rebuilt since the days of the Templars, but it is a faithful replica of the original building.

It is also said that in the 18th-century the entire male population of Temple was hanged for sheep-stealing. Only the knowledge that there were just two men living here at the time makes the story less horrific.

It was about this time too that John Wesley took on the task of revitalising the religion of England. During his evangelising journeys he visited Cornwall and its moor on many occasions. Once, he became totally lost when the features of the moor were blanketed with snow. He escaped by following the sound of the bells of Bodmin Church.The rooms where Wesley and his fellow-preachers stayed in Trewint now house a museum to this remarkable and dedicated man.

The moor around Minions and Caradon abounds with the ruins of a Bodmin Moor's more recent industrial history. Here the landscape is littered with decaying engine-houses of the 19th century. They give it an air of romance that was sadly absent when men and boys toiled thousands of feet below ground to earn a precarious living.

But walking on Bodmin Moor is far more than a stroll through Cornwall's history, fascinating though this is. Here the walker can see and hear the wheeling buzzard, marvel at the aerobatics of ravens and observe a wide variety of uncommon birds. There is always the chance, too, of coming face-to-face with badger or fox, or spotting the secretive stoat or weasel.

It is also easy for the walker in this still remote area to imagine that he, or she, might be the only person left on earth.

On this overcrowded island of ours there is a vital need to protect and preserve such oases of peace as this. By keeping to the designated routes the moorland walker can play his, or her, part in this aim and so ensure that the magic of the moor remains with us for ever.

Bodmin Moor can be all things to everyone who appreciates such areas of unspoiled beauty. I have told you of a few of my favourite places. Within the pages of this book, others share with you the places that are special to them.

Try the walks that are suggested. Visit the places they and I mention. Then, with the aid of an Ordnance Survey map, plan your own walks and discover Bodmin Moor for yourself.

Bodmin Moor is a wonderful locale for those who desire to walk and think their own thoughts, amidst the space and quietude existing in the very heart of this unique and special place that is – Cornwall.

TEMPLE Church which has a curious history.

WALK from ST BREWARD'S CHURCH to KING ARTHUR'S HALL

by Helen Wood

One of many extraordinary places on Bodmin Moor is King Arthur's Hall, possibly the site of an ancient temple, certainly a sheltered site of meeting in the middle of nowhere. This place of utter peace and stillness lies in a hollow on King Arthur's Downs, and is well worth the finding. It can be reached from a number of starting points, depending on how much walking you wish to enjoy before reaching your goal.

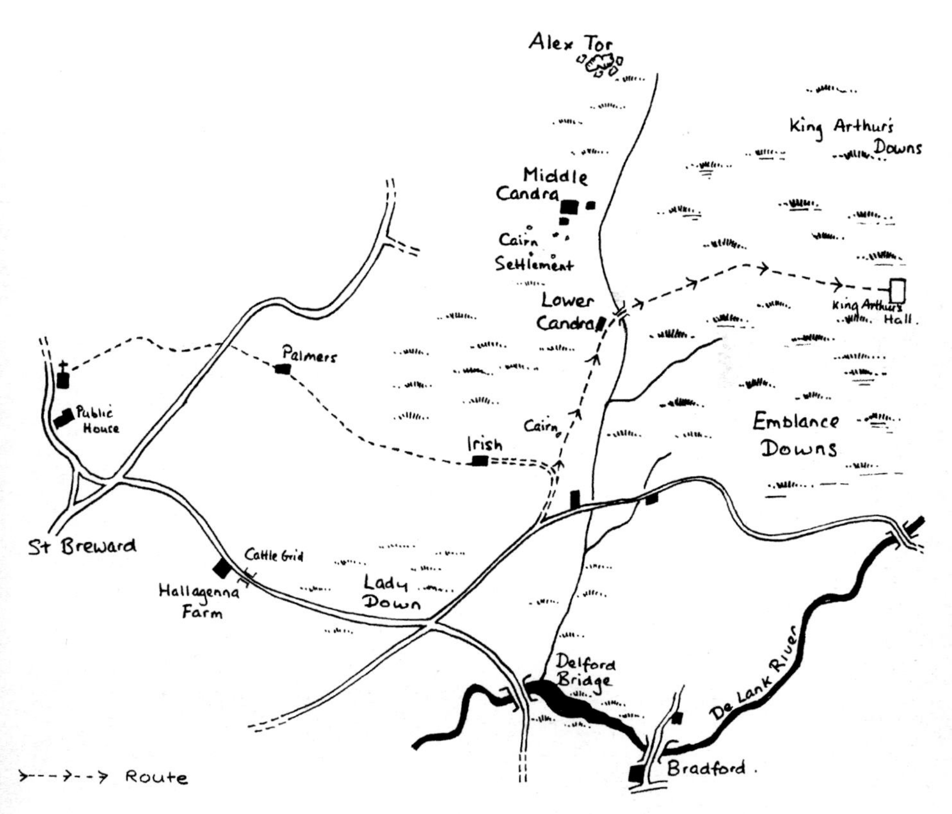

One beautiful spot to start is the church of St. Breward at Churchtown, north of St. Breward, reputed to be the highest church in Cornwall. This is Norman in origin, with remains of a Norman arcade; and, as Sir John Betjeman pointed out: 'By the time the fifteenth century granite tower, porch, south aisle and arcade were added, people had started to live and farm the wooded slopes of the Camel.' Betjeman remarked that the church still looks as it did when Thomas Rowlandson used it to illustrate Dr Syntax preaching, in the first volume of *Dr Syntax's Tour in Search of the Picturesque, 1812*. And, should you be fortunate with the weather, it has a lovely sundial.

The wide footpath, once you've passed the beech hedges of the graveyard, is embraced by shoulder-high granite-bouldered walls, under an avenue of beech trees, until you reach open land. However, I love the bleak vastness of the moor itself so advise driving further first, east beyond Hallagenna Farm with its riding stables, to leave the car at the side of the road, before heading up the track to the settlements of Irish and Lower Candra.

Here you join the footpath that started at Churchtown, and can immediately relish the views in all directions, and that distinctive underfoot texture of short rough grass and granite. Walking in early May, the only sounds are of skylarks that occasionally drop from the sky to disappear in the stone-strewn landscape, and the bleating of very young lambs huddled behind boulders against the wind which drains the sunlight of any warmth. The life up here, for man and beast, is harsh and always has been.

From Lower Candra the path drops to a stream bridged by huge granite slabs, a giant's fingers. The water rushes crisply over cress and, to the right, newly planted trees begin to soften the landscape. The path is clearly way-marked on each of the solidly constructed wooden stiles that straddle fence and stone hedge. Up the hill, through a maze of stone walls protecting the stock, until you are out on King Arthur's Downs and the path turns nearly due east to King Arthur's Hall. The walk takes less than an hour, and is relatively easy, though good boots are to be recommended in wet weather for the few areas of cattle-churned ground.

The Hall is fenced off from cattle and horses, but sheep are allowed in through a specially designed low entrance. You have another sturdy stile to climb and then you're into another world and time. Perhaps 22 metres by 50 metres, this vast rectangle is edged by raised banks from whose inner sides sprout standing stones which must once have provided respite from the winds. Some stand vertical, high as a man; some jut out at dangerous angles; yet others are prostrate. All are weathered smooth, and jewelled with lichens that change colour with the weather and time of day. Did they ever support a roof? Was it the meeting place of King Arthur and his men?

Larousse suggests the Arthur behind the myth was probably a Romanised Briton, possibly Ambrosius Aurelianus who lived in 'the turbulent century following the collapse of Roman rule in Britain (and) successfully commanded a mobile force of cavalry against Saxon invaders.' Certainly the animals most at home up here are the hardy moorland ponies, who barely notice your passing, their manes tossed by the wind. Maybe they are the descendants of Arthur's cavalry.

Whatever the historian's or archaeologist's answers, you can feel the sudden stillness as you step inside, out of the wind. And you can let your own imagination provide the answers. The middle of the Hall is now sunk into bog, and the brilliant reds and lush greens of this moist vegetation provide a fittingly rich carpet. It is a place to sit and dream.

What comes to my mind are lines from the mediaeval poem, *Sir Gawain and the Green Knight*, where Gawain, after long journeying and temptation, finds himself at the Green Chapel where he is due to be beheaded. The modern English paraphrase loses the alliterative strength of the Middle English, but still describes the place vividly: '... *he looked about him, and he thought it a wild spot, and there was no sign of shelter anywhere, only steep, high hills on either hand, and rugged, craggy rocks with rough outcrops; he thought the jutting crags grazed the clouds. Then, reining in his horse, he halted and looked every way, seeking the chapel.*

KING Arthur's Hall beyond St Breward. A lovely location which fires our speculation.

He saw nothing of the kind anywhere, which seemed to him strange, except, at a short distance across a glade, what looked like a knoll, a rounded mound on the side of a slope ... It had a hole at one end and one on each side, and was all overgrown with patches of grass, and quite hollow inside ..."now, truly," said Gawain, "this is a desolate place."'

And it is desolate. Once outside the protection of stone and bank, the wind howls. Perhaps these grouped standing stones were once the structural supports for a chapel or hall. Perhaps between and around them a domed structure was formed of smaller stones, like Celtic forts elsewhere. Or a roof could have been woven over the supple branches of willows from the numerous streams, and would have offered some protection from the elements – similar in design to those homes, called benders, of new age travellers.

Incidentally, the standing stones on the moor are not merely of historical interest. One good friend found himself at King Arthur's Hall when thick mist descended suddenly: he made his way home by following the standing stones, one more becoming visible as he reached the last. It is humbling to think for how long the stones may have served this important function to the inhabitants of the moor.

As you retrace your steps, sure of your route, record your surroundings sensuously if not mechanically. The moor is a mosaic of colours, starting from the tiniest wild violet or inch high pea of sun-filled gorse at your feet. Widen your vision to the grasses, reeds, and stone; to the willows of a freshly emerging rivulet, and beyond to the blues and greys of a skyline where stony Rough Tor and Brown Willy dominate. Hear the wind buffet your ears, locking in the skylarks and the bleating. And last, but not least, smell the honeyed wind and its freshness.

WALK from NORTH HILL to KILMAR TOR

by Guy Slatter

This walk appeals to me because it has something for everyone – fields, a river valley, deciduous woods, steep climbs, open moorland, a rugged tor and an element of pioneering along some stretches. There are, however, various alternative routes for you to follow, depending on your inclination and/or ability.

The walk starts in North Hill. Although there is no official car park in the village there are several places where you can park. I did so near the church, not far from the post office.

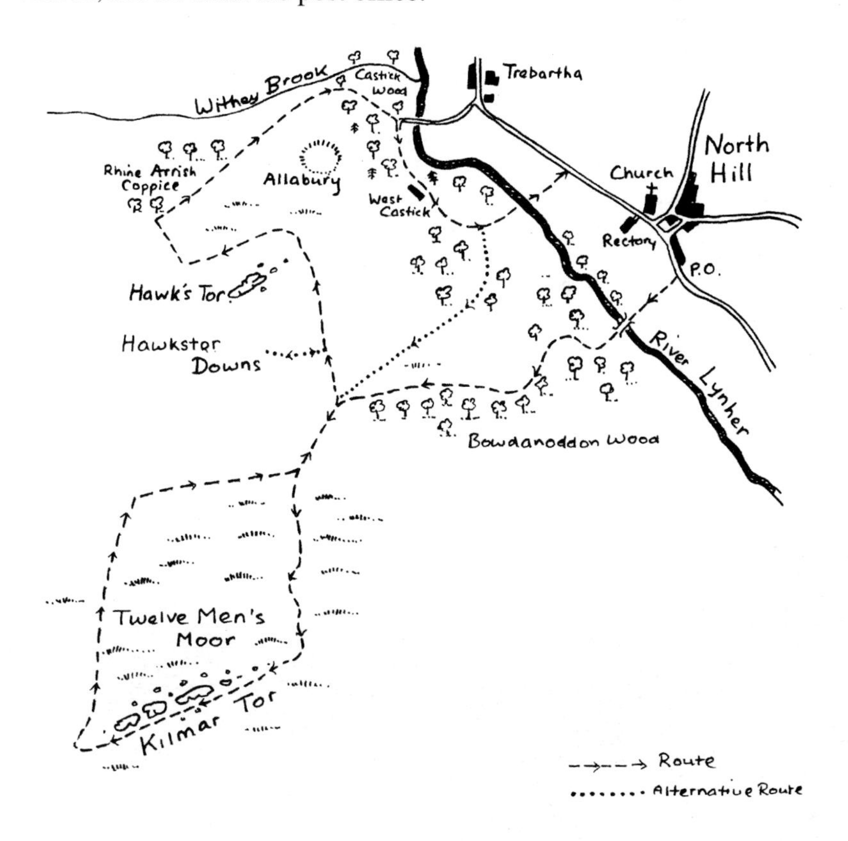

The public footpath starts about 100 yards on the right hand side down the road past the post office and is clearly marked. It goes round between two houses for a short distance before coming to a large kissing gate into a field. Go straight across the field, which begins to dip down into the Lynher valley. Although you cannot see the stile on the far side from the kissing gate it is obviously a popular walk, judging by the tracks in the grass. Once over the stile you descend a few steps before following the path diagonally down through a copse well-carpeted with bluebell plants. You cross a track and diagonally in front of you is a small narrow wooden bridge, followed a few yards later by a very fine, narrow, laminated wooden bridge across the Lynher. It is very pretty down there by the river.

At this point you have probably been walking for about five minutes.

From the river you head uphill and cross a stile into a field. Then there is a steep climb for about 250 yards, following alongside the bed of a stream. It is difficult initially, to see where you are heading, but if you make towards the gate at the top, just before you reach it you will see a stile behind some bramble bushes with a 'Public Footpath' sign. You cross a road. On either side of you are signs proclaiming 'No Access'!

Ahead of you, though, is another stile. Carry on uphill, beside the stream, which becomes quite a deep gulley near the top. There are more bluebells under the trees beyond it. At the top of the field, beside a kissing gate, is a Countryside Commission notice stating 'restoration work on this hedge is being carried out as part of a ten-year management agreement to ensure its long term future'. The people who erected the gate obviously assumed that, after climbing about 200ft since the river you will have lost weight, as it is rather small! Once through it you follow the hedge round to the left and very shortly emerge on a road. Here again the public footpath is clearly signposted. By this point you have probably been going for about 20 minutes.

Turn right and follow the road uphill – the gradient gets steeper as you go! On your left is a marvellous ancient stone wall enclosing the mainly coniferous Bowdanoddon wood and on your right, beyond the deep bed of the stream are first a beech wood and then fields. After about 15 minutes, having walked about half a mile and climbed a further 225ft you come to a gateway on the right with another 'Public Footpath' signpost.

Carry on past it, the road levels out, you reach the end of the wood and after about five minutes come to a gate across the road, in front of which there is room to park about a dozen cars. This marks the boundary with the moor proper.

You can, of course, drive to this point, saving yourself a walk of some 40 – 45 minutes, by taking the 'dead end' road at the west side of Berriowbridge.

A sign to your right at the parking place proclaims 'No access to Hawk's Tor summit – Private Land'. Beyond the gate the road/bridleway leads on across Twelve Mens' Moor between Hawk's Tor and Kilmar Tor. Another sign states: 'Bodmin Moor. This is a private agricultural common. No camping or fires. No vehicles to be driven off the highway. Dogs must be kept under control'. Twelve Men's Moor got its name because back in 1284 the Prior of Launceston granted a lease over it to twelve local men, one of whom was called Trewortha. That is still the name of the farm just over a mile away down the track ahead, lying beneath Trewortha Tor. Today the moor belongs to the Association of Bodmin Moor Commons' Landowners. Kilmar Tor lies in the middle of it.

Just beyond the gate an indistinct track leads off to the left, following roughly the line of the stone wall, towards the tor, which looms ahead. It is a long ridge, over half a mile long. To begin with the ascent is very gentle and it is not really until you start to climb up towards the eastern end that you can pick out the track, winding upwards through the boulders. It makes a left curve towards the summit of the ridge and at that point you can see Bearah Tor in front of you with Caradon Hill in the distance. Beside the track there are still weather-worn blocks of granite, cut out when stone was still being worked there. Once on the ridge it is an easy walk along it towards the fantastically-shaped boulders at the

AN angle of Kilmar Tor: one of the majestic features of the Moor.

top of the tor. It takes 20 to 25 minutes to get there from the car park. The trigonometry point marking the summit is a few yards to the west of the highest point (1299ft/796m), the third highest summit in Cornwall. A reasonably agile person can, with care, climb on to it. From the summit there are marvellous views across the moor in all directions, from Caradon hill and the north end of Siblyback lake to Rough Tor and Brown Willy and beyond. On a clear day it is possible to see Lundy island, 45 miles away.

From the summit you can either retrace your steps along the ridge or pick your way between the boulders and bilberry bushes and across the flat moorland, past some of the ancient cairns, heading straight for Hawk's Tor until you reach the track leading back to the gate where cars can park.

Retrace your steps along the road until you come to the gate with the signpost. Follow the rough track across the field – you are now on a bridleway – and shortly you will come across a Countryside Commission signpost with an arrow pointing to the left. Beware! If you follow it – initially along the old track leading westwards towards the old quarry under Hawk's Tor – after about half a mile you will come to a Countryside Commission Access site containing much evidence of historic features such as hut circles. The land in question is part of a government-funded conservation area and access to it is part of the agreement, being available until September 30, 2002.

If you ignore the arrow and carry straight on into the field ahead, you will be on the bridleway. Follow the line of the old wall to your left and in due course you will come upon an ancient narrow field gate giving access to the bridleway across the open moor. This section is very rough, but there are fine views over the Lynher Valley to your right. As the track turns westwards under Hawk's Tor it starts to descend, with rhododendron bushes on either side. Shortly, however, instead of carrying on beyond Hawk's Tor to complete the designated dog-leg, the track turns right, down into the field by Rhine Arrish coppice, where it rejoins the official route down the Withey Brook valley. By this time the walk will probably have taken about 25 minutes since you left the road.

By the gate leading on to the track down the valley there is an old granite pillar and a sign stating 'Public footpath – please do not stray'. It is a delightful track, by the side of the deciduous Cascade wood with its bluebells and primroses, which descends fairly steeply. At two places, where tracks come in from the left, there are white signposts clearly stating 'Public Footpath' or 'Private Forestry' for those coming the other way. It takes about 10 minutes to walk down the valley to where the track comes out on the road running from Trebartha round to West Castick farm. A sign on the gate through which you pass informs you that the woodlands are part of the Trebartha estate. At this point you could follow the road left to Trebartha and then to North Hill.

It is a pleasanter route, though somewhat more difficult , to turn right up along the road to West Castick. There you pass through the farmyard to the far side of the complex, where you should keep to the right of the hedge in front of you, following the route of an old cart track. Head for the gate at the bottom end of the wood in front of you. Having gone through it you have a choice. Either you turn left for North Hill or carry on back uphill towards the moor again.

If you choose the former, follow the hedge down to the gap at the bottom of the field into a large one adjoining the Lynher. Head for the marker/scratching stone in the middle and then towards the footbridge over the river. On the far side there is a short stretch of meadowland before the clearly visible path goes diagonally up the short wooded escarpment. There are some steps and a stile at the top bringing you into a field. From that point it is a steep 200 yards to the gate at the top, leading onto the road between Trebartha and North Hill. The path is clearly signposted on the road and is about 1/4 mile from the centre of North Hill. Using this route would take you about 1 hr 30 mins from where you started on the bridleway back to the village and the whole walk, including Kilmar Tor, about 3 hours. You can then regain your strength at the Race Horse Inn.

If you wanted to go back up on to the moor, or had started out on the latter path from North Hill, where the footpath meets the cart track between West and East Castick, follow along the bottom of the wood, across a stream and through a gate into a steeply sloping field. Head straight across it and on the far side you will pick up the track leading up into East Castick farmyard. The path is clearly marked on the far side of the yard. After a few yards up a track you enter a field. It is a steep climb across it to a stile leading into part of East Castick wood. Once inside the wood, follow the line of the wall on your right. Persevere along the somewhat overgrown path until you come to a stile at the top of the wood. This brings you out among some tall gorse bushes and rather boggy ground about 300 yards from the gate on to the road, which marked the start of the bridleway section. There is no clearly defined path, so you have to pick your own way. There is no danger of getting lost as the top end of Bowdanoddon Wood is clearly visible to the left of you. It is probably advisable to stay to the right of the stream until you join the bridleway near the Countryside Commission signpost. It would not be a good idea to try going the other way down the path to East Castick Farm. Setting out from North Hill by this route would take you about forty mins to reach the road at the top.

WALK from JAMAICA INN to DOZMARY POOL

by Michael Williams

Thanks to the superlative story-telling of Dame Daphne du Maurier, Jamaica is one of the most famous inns in all Britain. It stands just off the old coach road which ran across the moor to Bodmin.

When Daphne du Maurier first came here in the 1930s Jamaica was a Temperance House, 'hospitable and kindly' were her words. She and her friend Foy Quiller-Couch came on horseback. It was mid-November and

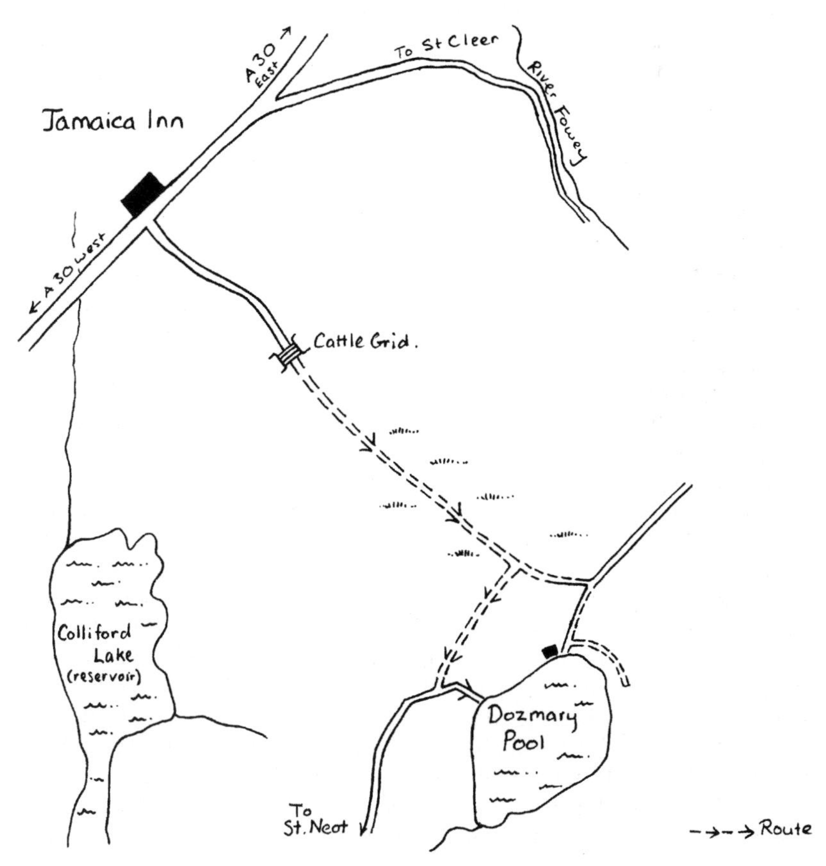

during the trip the young girls visited Dozmary Pool and the Cathedral of the Moor at Altarnun, where they met the local vicar. In the evening he came to visit them at Jamaica Inn, and they talked long into the night by the peat fire. Thus the seeds were sown, and *Jamaica Inn*, her great Cornish novel, began to grow in Daphne's sub-conscious.

Years later she wrote: '*But if, when you go there, you wonder whether the novel was pure fancy rather than expression of the spirit of the place as I saw it, take a walk behind Jamaica and, one morning before sunrise, climb Rough Tor and listen to wind and stones. Nothing has really changed since Mary Yellan walked the moors, climbed the tors, and rested in the low dips besides the springs and streams.*

Before you leave Jamaica Inn make sure you look at the Daphne du Maurier room which contains memorabilia from her last Cornish home Kilmarth near Fowey where she wrote *The House on the Strand* and her final novel *Rule Britannia*. Here you will see her writing desk on which there are an ancient typewriter, photographs, a packet of du Maurier cigarettes, named after her father the actor-manager Sir Gerald, and a dish of Glacier Mints, her favourite sweets.

As a member of the Ghost Club Society I have special interest in this inn because various paranormal activity has taken place here over the years. Reginald Carthew, who worked at Jamaica for more than half a century, told me he was often aware of being watched by an invisible somebody. A ghostly figure has been seen in one of the bedrooms and a number of people on different occasions have heard ghostly footsteps. Earlier in this century a stranger stood drinking at the bar but he never finished his drink. Called outside, he disappeared into the night. The next morning they found his murdered body out on the moor. The crime was never solved but years later a man was often seen sitting on the wall outside the inn. He never spoke and his description matched that of the murdered stranger.

The walk from Jamaica to Dozmary is only one and a quarter miles. The road is immediately opposite Jamaica's car park and it *is* largely a road walk, but once you get beyond the cattle grid the moor opens up at least on the lefthand side – and you begin to feel the freedom of the moor and the bleached grasses. Away to the right is another stretch of water: part of the man-made Colliford Lake.

Here in the moorland area cattle are usually grazing – interesting how many of them are black – like the peat of the moor. There are likely to be specks of black in the air too: crows in flight.

Just over a mile along the road swings right – to St Neot – like a C going the wrong way in that it starts from the bottom. On the bend take the track on your left. The odds are you will see more livestock. On my last visit a goat studied my progress down the track, a curious character. Out here you begin to appreciate these beautiful wide Bodmin Moor skies. On good days you get a lovely light and it is not surprising this part of Cornwall has inspired some very fine painting. Equally the Moor has fired the imagination of writers. Tennyson, Hawker and 'Q' all wrote about the Moor as have Charles Causley, James Turner and, more recently and very significantly, EV Thompson. He made his breakthrough into the big time with his novel *Chase the Wind*, first published in 1977, which will surely go down in literary history as one of the great novels to have grown out of the Moor. EV Thompson's characters live on in the reader's mind long after the book is closed – and that does not happen very often.

But back to the here and now and our walk.

Suddenly before you lies one of the great jewels of Cornwall, and on a sunny day it sparkles literally.

Dozmary is a beautiful sheet of water, often silent but always full of mystery and magic. Its strange beauty makes this a natural setting for folklore. Almost inevitably legends concerning Tregeagle and the sword Excalibur have developed out of this moorland oasis.

CE Vulliamy, touring Cornwall, in the 1920s, perceptively wrote: *'It could not be otherwise. The very passage of cloud and shadow, of mist and darkness over its face, the luminous forms that move phantasmally over its waters, would suggest miracles and marvels to the least imaginative mind.'*

AN old photograph of Jamaica Inn which is one of the most famous inns in all Britain.

Of Dozmary, Vulliamy said: *'Nowhere else on earth are there landscapes more austerely beautiful, more wonderful in their changes of mood and colour, or more splendid in outline. The Pool in its placid moods, when it becomes a mirror reflecting the forms of moor and cloud, has a charm so powerful, yet so elusive, that it can only be conveyed to you in pictures: the limits of descriptive writing are soon exhausted.'*

John Tregeagle, an unjust steward, was charged – by the spirits – for his misdeeds, and was sentenced to bail out Dozmary with a leaky limpet-shell. Tregeagle was so tortured by the impossibility of his task that he fled to Roche Rock, where, hammering and howling on the door of the chapel, he begged the Saints to grant him forgiveness and admission. Children of past generations were told that storm noises were really Tregeagle and his hell hounds out hunting. Hence the old Cornish expression: 'Howling like a Tregeagle'.

There are Arthurian echoes hereabouts in that some say Dozmary is where Sir Bedivere grudgingly threw away the wonderous sword Excalibur. Legend has it after the battle of Camlann, Sir Bedivere carried the dying Arthur away and Arthur ordered Bedivere to throw the sword Excalibur into a lake close by. Bedivere hesitated, reluctant to throw away such a sword, and hid it instead. When he returned to the King, Arthur asked him what he had seen. 'Nothing', answered Bedivere. Arthur knowing that his instructions had not been carried out, ordered him once again to do his bidding. Once again, Bedivere tried to fool the King. But the third time he did as he was asked. As the sword arced over the lake, *'there came an arm and a hand, and took it and cleight (seized) it, and shook it thrice and brandished, and then vanished with the sword into the water.'*

About 900 feet above sea level, Dozmary in winter can look an eerie place with mist covering its farther shore. There was an old belief Dozmary was bottomless – then in 1859 it dried up revealing a quite shallow depth – yet here on the rim of Dozmary you can feel the thrill of discover – or rediscovery. Speculation quickens. For all its fame the Pool remains part of Secret Cornwall.

◀ *DOZMARY Pool under a beautiful wide moorland day.*

WALK from ST CLETHER CHURCH to ST CLETHER HOLY WELL

by Jane Talbot-Smith

Leaving your car at St Clether Church, well worth a look for the Hardy connection, walk on through the churchyard and through the small gate and then follow the white posts, leaving the granite outcrops on your right. The Holy Well will quickly come into sight on the south-facing side of this delightful moorland valley of the young River Inny. The Well, built on a pre-Christian site, was adopted by St Cleder, one of several Welsh missionaries who came to Cornwall. With the coming of the Normans, who moved their site of worship, the Well and Baptistry fell into decline but were restored in 1879 and are the best example of chapel and well to survive in Cornwall. In more recent times the buildings have been repointed and fenced to keep the stock out. The footpath continues up this quiet valley following the course of the river before joining the road. On reaching the road you can either turn right and return to your car along the road or you can retrace your route back down the valley.

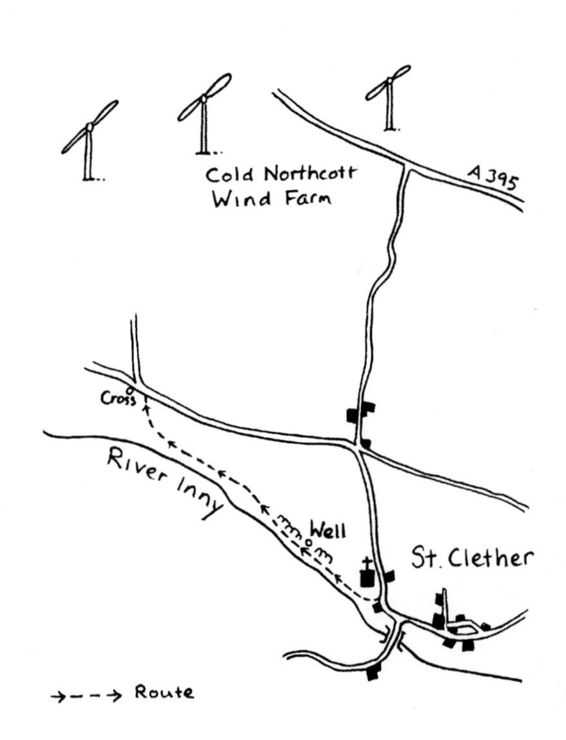

BOYS playing cricket on the only village green in Cornwall at Blisland. The churcb is a Cornish gem.

JUBILEE Rock

WALK from BLISLAND VILLAGE to JUBILEE ROCK

by Jane Talbot-Smith

Leaving Blisland village and taking the road to St Breward and Pendrift, at the crossroads turn right and after crossing the cattle grid park your car, taking care not to obstruct the cattle grid gate – for use of horse-drawn vehicles. The footpath is marked from this cattle grid and one scrambles over the bank before finding a well trodden track across the moor following the line of the hedge. After approximately a quarter of a mile you will see Jubilee Rock below you. Jubilee Rock was carved in 1810 to celebrate 50 years of King George 3rd. Lieutenant John Rogers came to Blisland with a recruiting party in October of that year, he was well-known in the village being the son of John Rogers of Pendrift, one of the church wardens. It is to John Rogers designs of Britannia and The Royal Arms on the front, are ascribed together with the arms of The Duke of Cornwall and Sir Arscott Molesworth on the sides, with other emblems of Industry, Agriculture, Plenty and Commerce as well as some Masonic Insignia that are carved all over the rock. Originally it appears the carvings would have been painted, but later they may have been picked out in black. Sitting on the rock you get extensive views to the west and can easily pick out the Padstow estuary and the China Clay pits of St Austell, whilst moving round to the north the view is obscured by Hantergantick Quarry. For the more intrepid the footpath continues to the de Lank river below with an enchanting valley to explore.

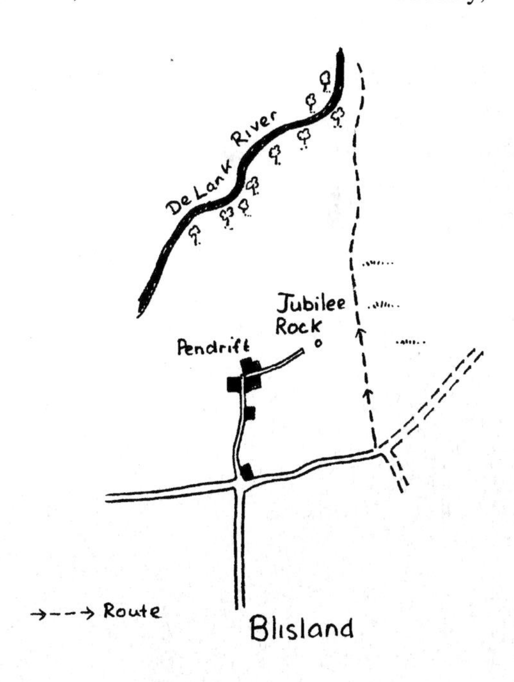

WALK at GOLITHA FALLS

by Jane Talbot-Smith

Golitha Falls were first mentioned in the Domesday Book and remain today one of the best beech woods on the edge of Bodmin Moor, well worth a visit. English Nature took over the management of the woods in the early 1990s since when they have had working parties to improve and maintain the pathways which are now well laid out and marked. The policy is to manage the woods and to protect the lichen, mosses and ferns which flourish in the damp atmosphere; bird boxes are in abundance and butterflies are actively encouraged.

Leaving the car park you have a choice of two routes to walk. The more level walk meanders between the river and the course of the old leat, between the beech trees which can be seen in their true magnificence. The falls themselves are a little disappointing having been blasted in the seventies, after the construction of Siblyback reservoir, to create a salmon passage to allow for their return upstream to spawn.

The second of the two walks is the more energetic as it rises up through the coppiced oak plantation to the top of the woods; and is aptly named the Bluebell Walk for the carpet of blue seen in the spring. The oaks were regularly coppiced up to the second world war, the wood being used for bean poles and to feed the fires of the charcoal burners, the charcoal going to the local mines. From the top of the woods the path descends to the falls and then returns to the car park along the river.

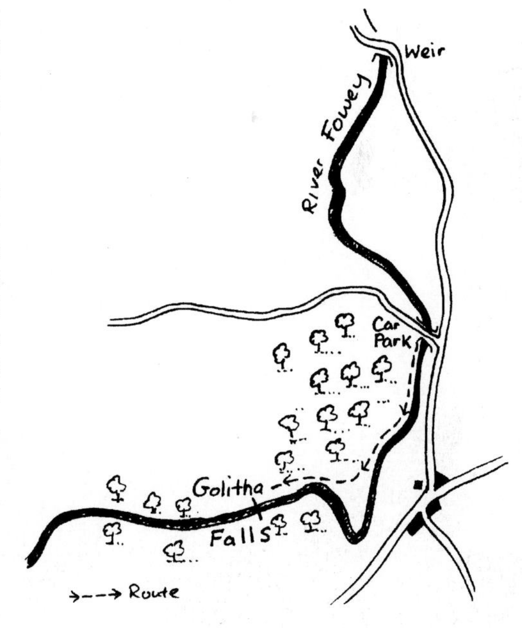

GOLITHA Falls: a place of beauty and refreshment.

Some Moorland Advice from Jane Talbot-Smith

- *Please do not undertake any of the walks in uncertain weather, for even those of us bred on the moor can lose our bearings when the mist comes down.*
- *Please keep your dogs under control at all times. Even if you know your dog will not chase sheep, the sheep do not know and any strange animal can make them bunch and run, which can lead to fatal accidents.*
- *Please take all your litter and rubbish home with you, the moor is a beautiful unspoiled area and we would like to keep it in its pristine condition.*
- *If in doubt about private land I would suggest you go to the local farmhouse and ask permission to walk, this gives the farmer a chance to advise you of where there might be dangers.*

JANE Talbot-Smith drives the novelist E V Thompson along the Fowey Valley below Jamaica Inn. Jane, who was the first Master Saddler in Cornwall, runs Higher Harrowbridge Saddlery two miles south of the A30 from Bolventor on the St Cleer road.

WALK from HURLER'S HALT, MINIONS, to the CHEESEWRING, on to DANIEL GUMB'S CAVE and the HURLERS STONE CIRCLE

by Donald Jackson

This walk starts from and finishes at the Hurler's Halt restaurant, a recent and much needed addition to the amenities of Minions as the many entries in their visitors' book testify. The first part – approximately 1.5 miles – is on metalled road so that those no longer able to walk on rough terrain can still enjoy some of the wonderful scenery by car.

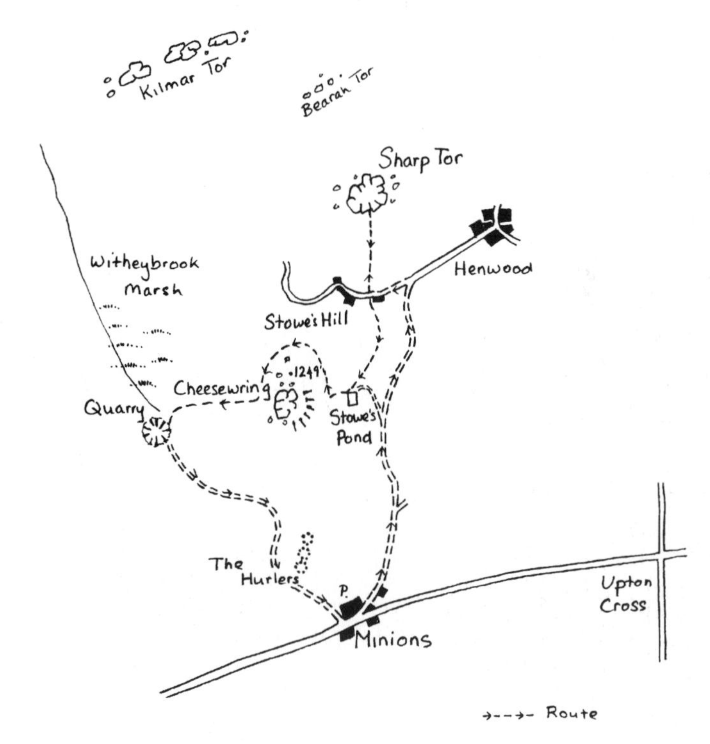

Let us start then at the Hurlers Halt – turn left on to the Upton Cross Road out of the village then left again after a couple of hundred yards on to the Henwood Road which winds down over the moor towards the village of Henwood. To my mind this is as beautiful and interesting a small road as one is likely to find throughout the length and breadth of the British Isles, but perhaps I'm prejudiced!

After a short distance on this road one becomes quickly aware of the Prince of Wales mine building which for some distance seems to be ahead until one finds the road veering to the left and it is seen to be down a track leading off to the right. This is arguably the finest engine house left standing in Cornwall albeit the youngest, being the remains of an abortive attempt to reactivate the mining wealth of the area at the beginning of the century. It became largely defunct at the time of the 1914-18 war. Until very recently it was a thing of great beauty with much of its surface clad in a thick coat of ivy which provided habitat for a great deal of wild life. For myself and many artist friends it was a joy to paint. It has now been stripped of its ivy and clumsily plastered with mortar in order to preserve the fabric and render it safe for visitors. It remains a majestic edifice, enormously interesting and well worth a special visit. I am assured that the ivy will return in due course but, until it does, it only remains paintable from a distance.

VIEW OF SHARP TOR FROM STANBEARE

Up to the left at this point one sees the outline of Stowe Hill and the Cheesewring Quarry and further ahead the aptly named Sharp Tor which we will examine closer as the walk progresses. Indeed Sharp Tor dominates the skyline throughout the entire length of the Henwood road and presents changing aspects of itself as the road twists and turns in its descent over the moor. My favourite view is from the cottages at Stanbeare (as shown in my pen sketch). For some distance prior to this point one can look eastwards (to the right) across East Cornwall and West Devon and, on a clear day, see the high ground of Dartmoor some 20 miles distant. When I look at this view on a dreamy summer day I never fail to feel an uplifting of the spirit, even after 20 years association with the area. Those who fail to be so moved, I can only assume, must have had their emotions cauterised.

Just as the road swings right on its final short descent into Henwood a No Through Road turns sharply back to the left. This is the road to Sharp Tor cottages although the sign had been removed at my last visit. Possibly some brainless wag with a mistaken idea of what constitutes humour perhaps? Be that as it may the road climbs quite steeply at this point through a collection of former miners' cottages which, when the mining was at its height in the second half of the last century, offered shelter to far more bodies than they do today. It is very difficult now, looking at these smart and tranquil dwellings, to imagine the congestion, squalor and deprivation that existed then. Suffice to say the expectation of life was considerably shorter and far less pleasant. This short steep road terminates at the entrance to a private farm road so it is hoped that a certain amount of consideration will be exercised and respect shown for the farmer's privacy.

It is at this stage of the walk that we have a choice, either to turn back left on the line of the old railway track that skirts Stowe Hill or to take approximately another half an hour to climb to the top of Sharp Tor itself which, for the more energetic, is well worth the effort. Having persuaded you to this effect we now cross diagonally right to a five-barred drover's gate and proceed to walk along the cattle track (having closed the gate behind us). This track can be extremely muddy after a spell of wet weather so beware, but don't let it deter you. After a few hundred yards there is a gap in the hedge to the left and through which the ascent to the top is immediately obvious following, as it does, roughly the line of the Cornish stone hedge. The scramble to the top takes approximately ten minutes but

SUMMIT STONES — STOWES HILL

once there the view on every side is breathtaking, with Bearah Tor and Kilmar Tor to the north and on the eastern slopes, at the right time of the year, signs of field divisions dating back, possibly, to neolithic times. For the purpose of this walk we have snatched a brief moment at the top of this impressive tor, but one could well spend more time in this area alone, exploring the traces of bronze and stone age men, such as hut circles, cairns and other field boundaries.

We now retrace our steps to the previously mentioned railway track and commence to follow this round the base for approximately a quarter of a mile where we can climb the side of Stowe's Hill to the summit, picking our way over the dry stone ramparts known as Stowe's Pound, believed to have been erected in the Bronze Age. Some say as defence against attacks by marauding neighbours and others that they were just village boundaries to contain livestock. Certainly there is ample evidence of a thriving agricultural community on these high slopes some three to four thousand years, and even more, ago with the remains of numerous hut circles on the northern slopes as well as a larger village boundary in addition to Stowe's Pound itself.

Over thousands of years the elements have eroded and fashioned the granite hill top into fantastic shaped boulders which lie around as though it were the deserted studio of some titanic sculptor and part way down the slope stands the pile of stones known as the Cheesewring – from its resemblance to the stones used in the making of cider to crush the apple 'cheese'. There they balance, impossibly, on the edge of the quarry like some giant stone sentinel at the ever-open gate of time and, if I am lucky enough to be there when few visitors are about, the imagination takes over and I conjure up mind pictures of what these stones have witnessed through the ages. The crude huts stand once more, the smoke from cooking fires billows in the wind and the smells from the pots assail the nostrils. The men of the village tend the lean moorland cattle and till their small plots whilst mischievous children run around prattling in a strange Celtic tongue ignoring, as children ever have done, the scoldings of their mothers! Or, moving closer to our own time, the brief half century or so, when the mining was at its height and the grunt, thud and grind of industry shattered the peace of the moor and small steam trains shunted and bumped in

the valley below as they carried the wealth that was South East Cornwall down to the port of Looe for shipment.

All this has passed away, never to return, and what we see now as we survey the slopes of Stowe's Hill is a random sprinkling of commoners' sheep, a few cattle and the odd pony or two. Man came and savaged the moor for a mere blip in historical terms, but nature has painted it with a healing brush, for which we are eternally thankful.

Before leaving Stowe's Hill we must survey the surrounding countryside as the views defy description. On the Henwood Road we can see eastward across to Dartmoor, the view enhanced by the extra height and, on a clear winter day, when the visibility is best, one can see over 40 miles to the beginnings of Exmoor. Tracking round to the right one can see Plymouth at a distance of some 18 miles and further round one sees the south coast of Cornwall and the Eddystone Lighthouse. To the west at 18 miles are the contours of the St Austell china clay tips, their ugly whiteness now tempered, in recent years, by a naturalising process which produces a covering of vegetation. Further north lies Brown Willy (the highest point in Cornwall at 1,375 ft) at some eight miles distant; due north one sees Sharp Tor behind which is the saw-edged outline of Kilmar Tor. The contrast of hazy distant views against dramatic foreground rock shapes offers numerous subjects for the artist to paint and the permutations of atmosphere are endless.

Turning our gaze again to the west we see in the middle distance, across the Witheybrook, a stone quarry which, from this viewpoint, looks like a small eruption on the face of the moor and to this we head now as there is another surprise in store. Before we do, however, we must take a look at one last fascinating feature. Picking our way down the western edge of the quarry there is a small hollow in the side of the hill to the right in which are the remains of Daniel Gumb's stone shelter. Not in their original position but re-erected to save them from the effects of quarrying in the nineteenth century. Daniel Gumb was an eighteenth century stone cutter and philosopher who chose to bring his family up on the moor away from the distractions of the rest of humanity. Finding a suitably sited large capping stone he hollowed out an artificial cavern beneath, creating several rooms so the current remains are but a fraction of the original. The remnant of capping stone has a geometric design carved upon it which I have heard variously described as a Euclidean problem and a proof of Pythagoras' theory, but I'm no mathematician – take your pick. There is also a stone nearby with the inscription 'D Gumb 1735' the significance of which date will probably stay for ever an enigma.

Having titillated our imagination with this strange tale we now head

across the Witheybrook to the 'Golddiggings Quarry'. As the quarry was created purely by the extraction of granite I am at a loss to explain how it acquired this particular appellation, although small amounts of gold have been found on Bodmin Moor.

Climbing the slope to the left of the waste heap we come to the quarry road and turn right where we are suddenly aware of something surprisingly beautiful. The cliff faces created by blasting have become naturalised and lying at the foot is a large limpid lake which is so deep (approximately 60 ft) that, although the water is crystal clear, it is impossible to see to the bottom. There is a secondary lake further in and the rocky ledges and grassy banks make this an excellent place to stop for a picnic lunch. It has unfortunately become somewhat over-popular of late and a minority of visitors leave their post prandial detritus behind as a testament to their ignorance. It would appear that some sensitive souls clear up from time to time as the rubbish never reaches unmanageable quantities, which restores my faith in human nature.

We now commence the last stage of the walk taking the road back towards Minions. Just under a mile along this quarry road and just before reaching the village of Minions itself, we see to the left the remains of the three adjacent stone circles known as 'The Hurlers', so called as they are said to be all that is left of a group of villagers turned to stone for playing the game of hurling on the Sabbath. One can think of certain groups today to whom such a sanction could be applied with advantage. More seriously, there has been endless conjecture as to what purpose these stones were erected. If one walks amongst them with dowsing rods they certainly behave very strangely and the ancient people undoubtedly were more in tune with the elemental forces of life than modern man. It, therefore, seems entirely possible that they had some mystical significance. Or perhaps they were some kind of cosmic calendar by which the moorland dwellers regulated their lives. It is unlikely that we shall ever know. From my own point of view they make an excellent subject for painting, particularly when one looks through them to the south over the silhouettes of the South Caradon mine ruins. If one is lucky, on a cloudy morning, one will see the sun glinting down through the clouds on the distant ocean, forming a silver strip across the horizon which is absolutely magical. At other times the sea is not visible but it is still a haunting scene.

PAINTER and book illustrator Felicity Young of Tintagel looks across to Brown Willy from Rough Tor.

WALK from ROUGH TOR FORD CAR PARK to the SUMMIT of ROUGH TOR

by Felicity Young

Rough Tor on Bodmin Moor, together with its slightly higher companion Brown Willy, dominates the skyline as you approach Camelford from either north or south. It stands at 1311 feet above sea level, so it is no wonder the walk to the summit is both challenging and exhilarating. The panoramic views exceed one's expectations; the silence, the isolation, the inexplicable atmosphere flood the senses and leave the walker with a feeling of wonder at one of Nature's most amazing creations in the Westcountry.

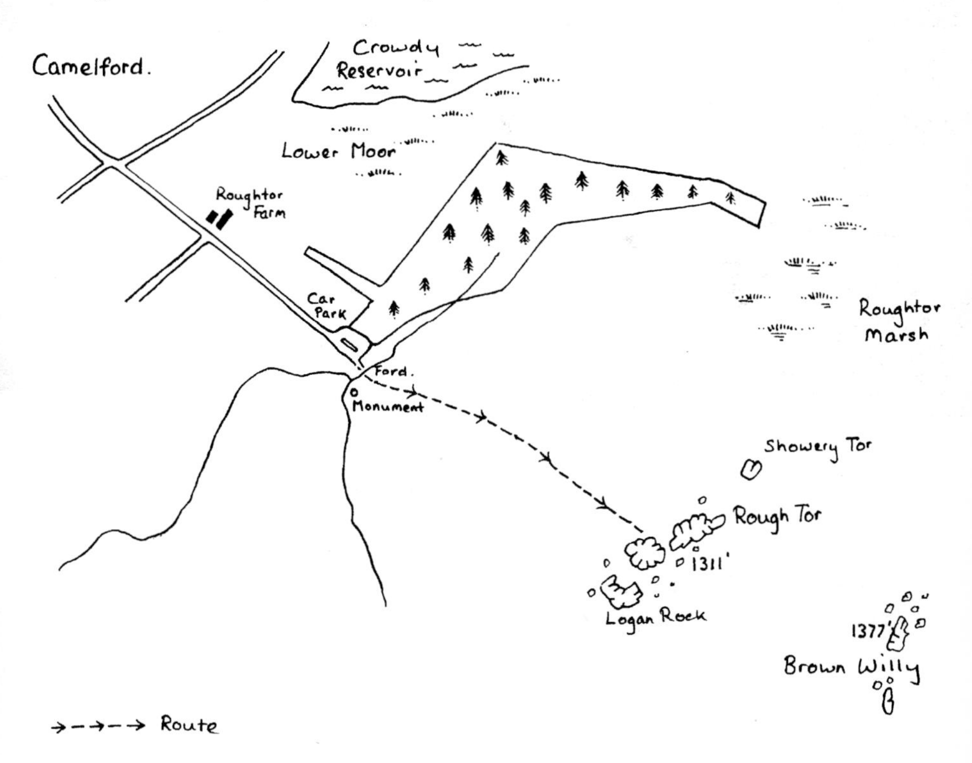

This immense pile of rocks is made up of highly individual stones, each one its own peculiar shape but playing a vital role within the structure. The overall appearance is one of instability, the stones precariously perched ready to tumble at any time, but of course it is more permanent than anything we can imagine, having stood here since the dawn of time. Human nature is such that if we see a hill it has to be climbed and Rough Tor is there just waiting to be 'conquered', to be experienced and enjoyed.

On leaving the carpark at Rough Tor Ford and passing through the gate beside the cattle grid you become immediately aware that you are entering an entirely different world. The scenery is bleak, a few sheep, wild ponies and cattle graze the short, springy turf. The grass is yellowy brown, typical of the moorland but on close inspection yields tiny wild flowers which are brave enough to withstand that often biting wind. A tributary of the river Camel flows under a stone bridge here, the ford is a popular watering hole for the livestock residing on the moor. It is important to remember the ponies are wild and not used to being handled by people; feeding them titbits is unwise as they can become aggressive when you run out of food! So keep your dogs under control and children close by when walking near the animals and the moor will continue to be somewhere where walkers can explore and experience a sense of freedom.

On the right of the gate where the river bank is flat there stands a memorial to a young girl. Charlotte Dymond was murdered here by her jealous lover one Sunday in 1844 as she was walking home. This bleak spot somehow seems very appropriate to remind us of such a hideous cold-blooded crime. Given the unusual atmosphere of the place it would not be hard to believe the accounts of the sentries of the Old Volunteers, once encamped nearby, who said they had seen the ghost of the poor unfortunate girl. But the feelings which you get from Rough Tor are by no means bad feelings, it is a magical place where the noise and bustle of everyday life are left far behind, the silence is one of its most intriguing qualities, just the wind stirring and the sound of the birds bring home one's own mortality. It is a place to go to be 'grounded', to be at peace with oneself, to be enveloped in the spirit and mystical atmosphere of this little corner of Bodmin Moor.

From the river the route is fairly obvious though the only definite tracks are those worn away by the sheep as they traverse the moor.

◀ *FELICITY Young at work by Charlotte Dymond's memorial.*

Upwards and onwards is the main criterion; the aim is to reach the summit of Rough Tor by as direct a route as possible. The final climb up through the rocks is quite taxing but well worth the effort as, once there, you can look over to Brown Willy in one direction or back towards Camelford with nothing to interrupt the view save the orderly drives of conifers or the boulder-strewn valley and far-off moorland. The summit is owned by the National Trust.

On the summit of Rough Tor is another memorial. A bronze plaque dedicated to the men of the 43rd (Wessex) Division remembers those who were lost on Hill 112 (Cornwall Hill) in Normandy in the Second World War. The 5th Battalion of the Duke of Cornwall's Light Infantry was virtually wiped out on this hill but the Cornishmen who survivied said 'This bloody hill looks like Rough Tor'. Every year a pilgrimage is made to the top of the Tor, prayers are said and the standards raised in memory of those who died in that fierce battle in France. For those who are not able to make the walk a tractor and trailer provides transport and soup and pasties make this annual event something of a celebration of the lives which were spared as much as a tribute to those brave soldiers who died.

All around Rough Tor is the evidence that the area was once inhabited by Bronze Age settlers. There are hut circles, tumuli and stone circles dotted about the lower slopes. It is not easy to identify these as you walk across the terrain but you may be aware of just a slight rise or a row of mounds, the clue that ancient people once made their homes here on this exposed and inhospitable land. Rough Tor, when seen from the car park does not appear to be any great distance, but it is one of those cases where, however long you are walking it never seems to get any closer! The huge pile of rocks looms ahead, other walkers on the same journey appear as tiny specks in the distance until suddenly you are at the base of the Tor itself and your fellow explorers are lost amongst the boulders above you. It is only when standing close to these stones you realise just how huge they are, dwarfing any human being who dares to stand near these monuments of the landscape. Rough Tor is a great experience – and place.

AND, WHEREVER YOU GO, FOLLOW THE COUNTRY CODE

Enjoy the countryside and respect its life and work
Guard against all risks of fire
Fasten all gates
Keep your dogs under close control
Keep to public paths across farmland
Use gates and stiles to cross fences, hedges and walls
Leave livestock, crops and machinery alone
Take your litter home
Help to keep all water clean
Protect wildlife, plants and trees
Take special care on country roads
Make no unnecessary noise.

SOME PLACES OF INTEREST ON BODMIN MOOR

THE CATHEDRAL OF THE MOOR at Altarnun

PENHALLOW MANOR, a country house hotel at Altarnun, used by Daphne du Maurier in her famous novel *Jamaica Inn*.

JOHN WESLEY'S COTTAGE at Trewint, a Methodist shrine.

THE NORTH CORNWALL MUSEUM and GALLERY on the edge of the moor at Camelford.

HURLER'S HALT for food and drink at Minions in the heart of the old mining country. Exhibits and sells paintings by Donald Jackson.

HIGHER HARROWBRIDGE SADDLERY at Bolventor – work also includes craft boxes, belts and bags.

THE OLD INN at St Breward, one of the highest inns in all Cornwall.

HELLAND POTTERY operated by Paul Jackson a distinguished Cornish potter.

THE FOWEY VALLEY below Jamaica Inn, a delightful walk or drive.

THE TRIPPET STONE CIRCLE on Manor Common.

COLLIFORD Lake, a 20th century lake formed to meet the needs of both residents and visitors.

More Bossiney Books

Daphne du Maurier Country

by Martyn Shallcross, who knew Daphne du Maurier for over 20 years and became a close friend. Illustrated in colour throughout, this new edition shows many of Dame Daphne's haunts and, with wonderful stills from the films made of her novels and short stories, mingled with personal photographs taken at Menabilly and Kilmarth, brings to life her rich and imaginative world.

About Tintagel

Stunningly situated Tintagel and its rugged castle conjure up colourful images of King Arthur and his court, but what really happened in this wild and beautiful place? Here we sift the archaeological and historical evidence in search of the truth. Colour photographs throughout.

About Hawker and Morwenstow

The northernmost tip of Cornwall is famous for its connection with the Rev. R S Hawker, its Victorian vicar and poet, who with his *Quest of the Sangraal* did almost as much as Tennyson to foster interest in King Arthur and the Tintagel connection. This book is about both the man and Morwenstow today.

Ghosts of Cornwall

Peter Underwood, President of the Ghost Club Society and celebrated ghost-hunter, relates strange happenings that cannot easily be explained by the laws of nature. Meeting fascinating people and hearing their intriguing accounts (and experiencing some strange phenomena himself) he retells their curious tales of spectral encounters.